Earthquake!

BY ELIZABETH RAUM

AMICUS HIGH INTEREST • AMICUS INK

Amicus High Interest and Amicus Ink are imprints of Amicus
P.O. Box 1329, Mankato, MN 56002
www.amicuspublishing.us

Library of Congress Cataloging-in-Publication Data
Raum, Elizabeth, author.
Earthquake! / by Elizabeth Raum.
    pages cm. – (Natural disasters)
Audience: K to grade 3.
Summary: "This photo-illustrated book describes how
earthquakes happen, how quakes affect people, and highlights
some historic earthquakes. Includes information on keeping safe
if living in an area prone to quakes"– Provided by publisher.
Includes bibliographical references and index.
ISBN 978-1-60753-989-6 (library binding)
ISBN 978-1-68152-082-7 (pbk.)
ISBN 978-1-60753-995-7 (ebook)
1. Earthquakes–Juvenile literature. I. Title.
QE521.3.R384 2017
551.22–dc23

                          2015031465

Editor: Wendy Dieker
Series Designer: Kathleen Petelinsek
Book Designer: Tracy Myers
Photo Researcher: Rebecca Bernin

Photo Credits: BluesandViews/iStock cover; Grant Smith/
CORBIS 4-5; Richard Ward/Exactostock-4268/Superstock 6;
Geoff Renner/Robert Harding World Imagery/Corbis 9; Guo
Jian She/Redlink/Redlink/Corbis 10; jamesbenet/iStock 13;
Bettman/Corbis 14; YOSHIKAZU TSUNO/Staff/Getty Images
17; ELIANA APONTE/Reuters/Corbis 18; Mark Pearson/
Alamy Stock Photo 21; think4photop/Shutterstock 22-23;
imageBROKER/Superstock 25; ERIK DE CASTRO/Reuters/
Corbis 26; epa european pressphoto agency b.v./Alamy Stock
Photo 29

Printed in the United States of America.

HC 10 9 8 7 6 5 4 3 2 1
PB 10 9 8 7 6 5 4 3 2 1

Table of Contents

Shaken Up

One minute everything is fine. Then the floor shakes. A picture falls off the wall. The walls make cracking sounds. Outside, a car horn honks. Did a car crash into the house? No. But it felt like that. What really happened? An earthquake shook the ground!

A home is cracked and broken after an earthquake.

This diagram shows how earth's surface is made of moving plates.

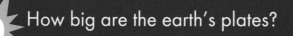

Q How big are the earth's plates?

The earth beneath our feet seems solid. But it's not. The earth is made of huge plates of rock. These plates are always moving. Most of the time they move very slowly. They slide past one another. Sometimes they rub together. Sometimes they crash. The crash is the start of an earthquake.

 They are as big as the continents. One is as big as the Pacific Ocean.

The place where the plates rub is called a **fault**. It's a break in the earth. At the edges of a fault, the plates are stuck together. Below ground, the rest of the plates try to keep moving. They can't. Pressure builds up. It sends energy in all directions. The energy makes the earth tremble or shake.

The land splits along this fault in Iceland.

An earthquake in China destroyed these buildings and everything around them.

Q How do earthquakes kill people?

How Bad Is an Earthquake?

There are about a million earthquakes around the world every year. About half of them are small. Some happen far from towns and cities or under the ocean. No one notices them. The other half are big enough to feel. About 16,000 quakes a year cause major damage. Some are killers.

 People die because buildings fall during an earthquake. Roads and bridges break apart. Fires begin when gas lines burst.

Scientists use a **seismograph** to measure the strength of a quake. This machine makes zigzag lines on paper. The lines show when and where a quake struck. It shows how much energy the quake gave off. Short lines mean small quakes. Big wiggly lines mean big ones.

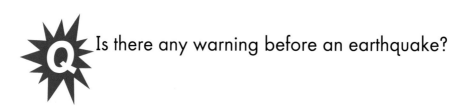 Is there any warning before an earthquake?

This machine measures how much the ground is shaking. Big wiggly lines mean stronger shaking.

A Not yet. Scientists cannot tell when an earthquake will hit.

Scientist Charles F. Richter studied earthquakes.

Q Do great quakes always do more damage than small ones?

Charles F. Richter was a scientist who studied earthquakes. He looked at the wiggly lines on the seismograph. In 1934, he created the **Richter Scale**. He started at 1.0. Small quakes measure 2.0 or less. We don't feel them. We feel quakes that are 4.5 or bigger. Quakes 8.0 or higher are called "great" quakes. Richter called these measures **magnitudes**.

 No. Some small quakes do major damage. Even a small quake can destroy poorly built roads and buildings.

After an earthquake, scientists use another measure. The **Mercalli Scale** measures how strong a quake feels to people. It measures the damage to homes, buildings, and roads. The scale shows which areas need the most help. It teaches city planners which buildings are safest.

The star marks a quake. Places closest to the star feel the quake the strongest.

Soldiers hand out water to people after an earthquake in Haiti.

 What's an **aftershock**?

Really Awful Great Quakes

On January 12, 2010, a magnitude 7.0 quake hit Haiti. Almost 300,000 houses fell apart. More than 220,000 people died. Another 300,000 were hurt. People had no water. They were hungry. Many got sick. There were 52 aftershocks. This made things even worse. Haiti is still rebuilding.

 Aftershocks are small quakes. They follow a big quake. They can continue for weeks, months, or years.

On March 11, 2011, a magnitude 9.0 quake struck under the ocean near Japan. It lasted six minutes. This big quake at sea caused **tsunami** waves. The waves flooded the land. The government warned people. But the warnings could not save everyone. More than 18,000 people drowned. The huge waves destroyed villages. The waves carried lots of **debris** out to sea.

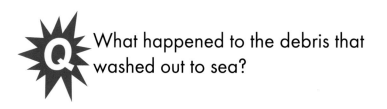
What happened to the debris that washed out to sea?

Tsunami waves destroyed these houses in Japan in 2011.

 Some of it sunk. Some has landed along the West Coast of North America. Some is still floating around in the Pacific Ocean.

In April 2015, a magnitude 7.8 quake struck Nepal. Nepal is a country in Asia. The quake destroyed towns. Houses fell. So did many ancient temples. People were buried under the debris. Nearly 8,500 people died. Shops closed. Power failed and there was no clean water. It will take years to recover.

People fill buckets with water after the quake in Nepal.

Saving Lives

One expert says, "Earthquakes don't kill people. Poorly built buildings do." Safer buildings save lives. Stone homes fall apart in a quake. They are stiff. Wooden or bamboo houses are safer. They move with the earth. Homes made of straw bales may be safest of all. They sway with the earth. Straw homes are cheap to build.

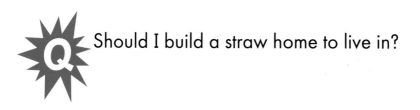 Should I build a straw home to live in?

Workers in Haiti build homes that will be stronger in an earthquake.

 No. In North America, homes in earthquake zones are built to be safe. In countries like Haiti and Nepal, straw homes can save lives.

Children in the Philippines have earthquake drills at school. They are ready to take cover.

Q Which U.S. state has the most earthquakes?

Be Prepared

Know what to do if a quake strikes. If you are inside, drop down and crawl under a desk or table. Hold on to the table and stay there until the shaking stops. If you are outside, go to an open field. A soccer field or a baseball field is safe. The biggest danger is falling buildings. Stay away from buildings in an earthquake.

Alaska has the most quakes and the biggest. Ten of the 12 biggest U.S. quakes were in Alaska.

Earthquakes can happen anywhere. Most do no harm. But people who live near big faults need to be prepared for a quake emergency. Know how to find your family. Have an **emergency kit** ready. It should hold first aid supplies, water, and food. Keep flashlights and candles handy. If trouble strikes, you'll be ready.

This road in San Francisco cracked in an earthquake.

Glossary

aftershocks Small earthquakes that happen after a large one.

debris Broken pieces of something that has been destroyed.

emergency kit Supplies that will be useful in a sudden, unexpected problem.

fault A crack in the earth where the plates rub together causing earthquakes.

magnitude The size or amount of something.

Mercalli Scale A way to measure how strong an earthquake is and the damage caused.

Richter Scale A way to measure the energy an earthquake releases.

seismograph A machine that measures the time, place, and size of an earthquake.

tsunami A huge wave that happens after an earthquake in the ocean.

Read More

Coleman, Miriam. *Investigating Fault Lines*. New York: PowerKids Press, 2015.

Collins, Terry. *Buried in Rubble: True Tales of Surviving Earthquakes*. North Mankato, Minn.: Capstone, 2016.

Stewart, Melissa. *Inside Earthquakes*. New York: Sterling, 2011.

Websites

National Geographic | Earthquakes 101
video.nationalgeographic.com/video/101-videos/earthquake-101

Northern Illinois University | Modified Mercalli Intensity Scale
elearning.niu.edu/simulations/images/S_portfolio/Mercalli/Mercalli_Scale.swf

PBS Kids | Earthquakes
pbskids.org/dragonflytv/show/earthquakes.html

Every effort has been made to ensure that these websites are appropriate for children. However, because of the nature of the Internet, it is impossible to guarantee that these sites will remain active indefinitely or that their contents will not be altered.

Index

About the Author

Elizabeth Raum has worked as a teacher, librarian, and writer. She says, "Storms are exciting." She has lived through blizzards and floods. She's seen a tornado in the distance. She watched earthquakes, hurricanes, and wildfires on the Weather Channel. It's safer! Visit her website at www.elizabethraum.net.